our warmest thanks
to the bahianian artists we met
and who guided and led us
throught the discovery of BAHIA.

our very special thanks
for their efficient contribution to:

Alfredo Machado of Distribution Record
who encouraged us to achieve this book

Phillip Hill for the English translation

Liliane Dubois of the Varig Company
for the numerous advice

Jean-Louis Delquignies of the Meridien Hotel
for his hospitality

Cristina Yanguas of the Meridien Hotel
who allowed us to be at the right place
at the right moment

our thanks also for their precious help to:
Paulo Gaudenzi, President of Bahiatursa
Luis Raymundo and Nicia Maria Tourinho Dantas
Daniel Vacher and Maria Oliveira Braga of Embratur
Gildeme Larsen of Bahiatursa
Carlos de Araujo Filho

The original edition of this book was realised in 1984 by the *Banco Frances e Brasileira,*
associated to *Credit Lyonnais*

Editions d'art Yvon, 30 avenue Jean-Jaurès — 94110 Arcueil — France

Distribuidora Record R. Argentina, 171 CEP 20921 Caila Postal — Rio de Janeiro

BAHIA

MYSTERY LAND

ALAIN DRAEGER-JORGE AMADO

The origins of the
town of Bahia are as-
sociated with magic
and love, inspiring the construction of the buildings and moulding
its way of life. It was in about 1510 — historians cannot agree on the
exact date — that a Portuguese explorer was shipwrecked on the
coast. Strong, intelligent and a good swimmer, he escaped
drowning and even managed to save his musket. His name was
Diogo Alvares. On the shore, the local Indians were there to greet
his arrival with enthusiasm : they were extremely partial to
succulent pieces of human flesh and particularly the flesh of whites
— a rare treat in those parts-and started making preparations to eat
him for lunch. Aware of the gravity of the situation, Alvares showed
great imagination ; already the breezes of Bahia, reputed to
produce clear thinking, were doing their work. Aiming his musket,
which had been saved so luckily, he shot and killed a bird flying
overhead. The detonation and flash from the gun blinded the
Indians and the dead bird induced fear in them.
« Caramourou ! Caramourou ! » they cried, saluting this son of
thunder, this master of fire and death, this queer and violent being
who came out of the water. They brought him succulent fruits,
lavished favours on him and heaped honours on to him. They gave
him the daughter of the chief, Paraguassou, to look after him, keep
him warm at night and pick his lice. Diogo Alvares thus started
living the life of a king off the riches of the land. He had made a
good deal.
From this turn of magic was born Bahia but its foundations were
built on a profound love.
The chief had another daughter, Moema, hardly yet adolescent, still
almost a child. In her heart rose up an intense passion for her

sister's man. From the first moment that she saw him coming out of the water like a silver fish, she fell in love with him. She loved even before she saw him spurt fire from his musket to kill the bird. She loved Diogo while he was still a weak castaway at the mercy of the Indians. She wanted to cover him with her naked breasts, to die with him at this critical moment. Then the stricken bird fell into her trembling hands and the blood ran between her fingers. The man from the water was not a defenseless creature. He was the god of fire, the master of thunder and lightning.

Moema's heart was consumed with desire but according to the custom it fell to the eldest Paraguassou to make up the bed of the white man and lie down with him. It was for the eldest to look after the guest and bear his children, to share his good fortune and the oad. Grievously wounded in the heart, Moema hid in the forest, a mighty flame devouring her soul.

One day, Diogo Alvares set sail with his wife aboard a small ship to visit the kings of Europe. They say he reached Paris where the Indian Paraguassou was baptised in the Catholic religion and named Catherine.

Moema, whose impassioned eyes followed Caramourou everywhere, watched in despair as the ship left, pushed by the wind, scudding past the island of Itâparica towards the infinite distance. Hopeless, she ran down the beach surrounded by birds.

What was the point of living if he was no longer there ? She threw herself into the sea and into the wake of the ship with its unfurled sails, she cried out the name of her love. With fish swimming all around her and her hair streaming, Moema swam after the disappearing ship which was carrying away the object of her love. The moon came out casting its gold and silver over the water. Way on the horizon the light of the boat was being eaten up, merging into the background of stars. But Moema kept on swimming although she was at the end of her strength.

When the light of the ship finally disappeared into the night, Moema felt herself losing the rest of her strength and gave herself up to die. Without Diogo she no longer wanted to live. She let herself go under with her cortege of fish and moon without her marriage veil. Since then and for ever more, the light of love shines on the sea and land of Bahia.

9

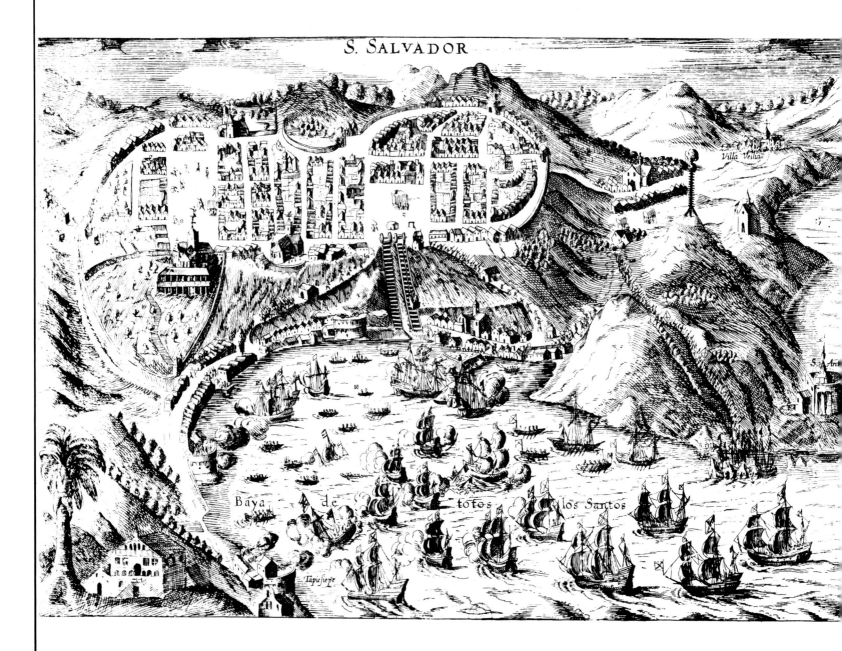

S. SALVADOR

São Salvador, city of the Saviour, in Latin Soteropolis or Civitas Sancti Salvatoris, capital of the South American country known as Brazil, is situated on the north side of the bay known to the Portuguese as the Bay of All Saints, a bay so large, so deep, so suitable and so safe that it has no equal in the world. It is because of this bay that the city is also called Bahia.

Taken from the "Grand lexique universel complet", Leipzig, 1740.

SALVADOR DA BAHIA

Here I would like to present a vision of the city of Bahia itself, its complex world, its strong humanism, its cultural originality. I would also like to talk about the country, of its naturel riches, of the riches the Bahians have created, and above all to talk about the Bahians.

Bahian means a native of Bahia, but the word also describes a state of mind, a certain conception of life, a particular form of humanism, open and creative — almost a philosophy. It explains why some men and women born elsewhere far from Bahia recognise that they are Bahian at heart from their very first contact with this land of the *saveiros,* with the roughness of the *Sertão* or the *vaquejadas* and its miracles, a land marked by the genius of its people so hard-working and cordial. The lucky ones who feel this are quickly accepted by the

Bahians themselves as authentic. The others who never succeed in becoming Bahians are not of interest to us here, only those from foreign climes who have acquired Bahian « citizenship » and have given us the precious contribution of their experience.

The most recent of these Bahians to come from elsewhere is Alain Draeger. He had hardly been there a moment than he was able to capture, through his camera, the body and soul of Bahia as if he had been born in this fairytale place which he shows with such beauty and which is now incorporated into his fine art. The text and photographs in this book echo the popular song of Dorival Caymmi, the most popular of Bahian composers :

« Have you ever been to Bahia, darling ? »

« No. »

« Then get there straight away ! »

The city rises out of the sea, guarded by the fort of São Marcelo, looking like an enormous tortoise or bizarre conch anchored in the gulf. The old fortress is part of the landscape and of history. It protected the town against invasions from the French and Dutch. It protected the town against invasions from the French and Dutch, it played an important role in the fight for independance, and it was a barracks and prison. Today it serves another purpose and will soon house the Museum of Maritime Commerce of the South Atlantic. This fort is the first thing a visitor sees arriving by ship and the last thing on leaving.

But more than this fort, more than the control posts on the main roads or at the airport, the town has a much more vigilant protector. At every entry to the city's

16

heart whether by old narrow streets or wide avenues, *Eshou* stands to guard its intimacy, its beauty and its mystery. He is one of the most important *orisha* of the *Candomble*. Often confused with the Devil in the syncretism with the Catholic religion because he is malicious and turbulent, he loves disorder and jokes. Posted at the crossroads of all the streets, hidden in the halflight of dawn or dusk, *Eshou* protects the town against anybody who comes with their heart filled with hate or brings with them violence. The Bahian people are gentle and cordial. *Eshou* bars the route to rascals and evil-doers.

When you first set foot in Bahia, the first thing you must do is to give *Eshou* a drink in order to be in his good graces. Any visitor who is about to drink alcohol would do well to offer the first mouthful to *Eshou* by pouring it discretely on the ground. He will thus find himself under his protection and all roads will be open to him — equally those that lead to the mystery and beauty of Bahia as those which lead to the hearts of women, these brown women of Bahia whose skin colour varies from ivory to copper but always confers on them an infinite charm.

Four and a half centuries have past since the famous Jesuit priest who came with the first colonisers' ships — the year the town was officially founded — wrote his manuscript. The hills which were almost virgin — there were only the huts of Vila Velha, the primitive village — have given way to a metropolis which undulates like

« The hills look like vast gardens and orchards — I cannot remember ever seeing such a beautiful tapestry. » Father Manuel da Nobrega, Jesuit Society, 1549.

a stranded fish on the shore for sixty kilometres from
the end of the bay with its calm waters to the beaches
beaten by waves from the Altantic Ocean. The land —
the temperature varies between 20 and 30° C. is fertile,
the climate agreeable — the sun shines all year round
and the rain, though frequent is brief and warm
washing the beautiful face of the city. The nature of
Bahia, rich and generous, makes life gentler — it forms
the basis of the beauty of Bahia.
Close to the port, safe and with easy access, the
Portuguese built huge houses, their walls covered with

20

stone slabs to resist the water, and large warehouses. At first they stored in these warehouses wood from the forest which at that time came right down to the settlement. Their preference was for the Brazil wood after which the new land was named.

On a sand spit, the Portuguese built the Fort de la Mar. At the top of the hill they established the political seat with the administrative palace, the first churches and on the edges of the town, to house the troops, they built other fortresses facing out to the sea to protect the merchant ships coming from Lisbon for wood, sugar and tobacco. In their holds as balast on the way out, the ships carried blocks of limestone and sculptures destined for the altars. With the crews came the first architects and experienced craftsmen. And priests as well, but no women.

The few streets, narrow and tortuous, were laid with raw stones. Thatch on rooves was progressively replaced by tiles and the houses fitted with floors.

Around the settlement, the colonisers built a two-kilometre long wall between the Benedictine monastery and the Carmelite monastery to keep out unruly Indians and invasions from foreign powers. In order to keep their Negro slaves docile and obedient, they erected a gallows and a pillory.

Still today, when the fortified town is only a memory in history books, the city has a Gallows Street and a Pillory Square. The harmony of the colonial architecture with its simple, clean design has been replaced by a disparity of styles added successively during the course of time, right up to the era of the skyscrapers with their vast walls of glass fitted between thin, cold

columns of concrete. Imposing mansions in the European style live side by side with modern buildings. The frenetic urbanisation of the outlying parts of the town has deprived the small houses of the poor of their gardens and allotments. Crowded together, the houses of the rich have as neighbours the misery of those of the poor. Time and the human hand have formed the many-facetted face of the city of today whose unity consists of a growing intermixing of styles.

With the aid of their blunderbusses, the Portuguese colonisers, who can not be described as the whitest of white, decimated the Indians who refused the forced labour and Catholicism, preferring to remain faithful to the free life of the forests. The indoctrinated Indian died in sadness or fell into listlessness. The Portuguese therefore went to Africa to bring back Negros. So began the infamous but lucrative slave traffic which was to last three centuries. The Negro took on to his shoulders the burden of servitude and despite his irons knew how to laugh and fight. It was in a north-eastern corner of Brazil that the first Negro republic came into being : Palmares. Neither racial differences, however, nor the difficulties of living under such a fierce regim whose white representatives held the power of life and death, nor the non-submission of the Indian and his genocide, nor the horrors of slavery, prevented the mixing of bloods. The Dutch and the French came too, occupying this new land for some time and leaving behind a trace of their blue eyes in the brown faces. The beauty of the city, was therefore enriched by unforeseen touches. Bahia was a meeting point of races and morals, the first capital of the land, rich and famous during the first centuries of the Brazilian nation, a port open to ships from the entire world, to people with the same ideas and to those with completely different ones. Bahia was propitious to cultural and religious syncretism, to the interpenetration of different sources and currents of thought. This mixture, parallel with white, black and indigenous blood, has become the dominating characteristic of the social panorama. It created here a strong, popular culture which is clearly shown in the various aspects of the flourishing life of the capital.

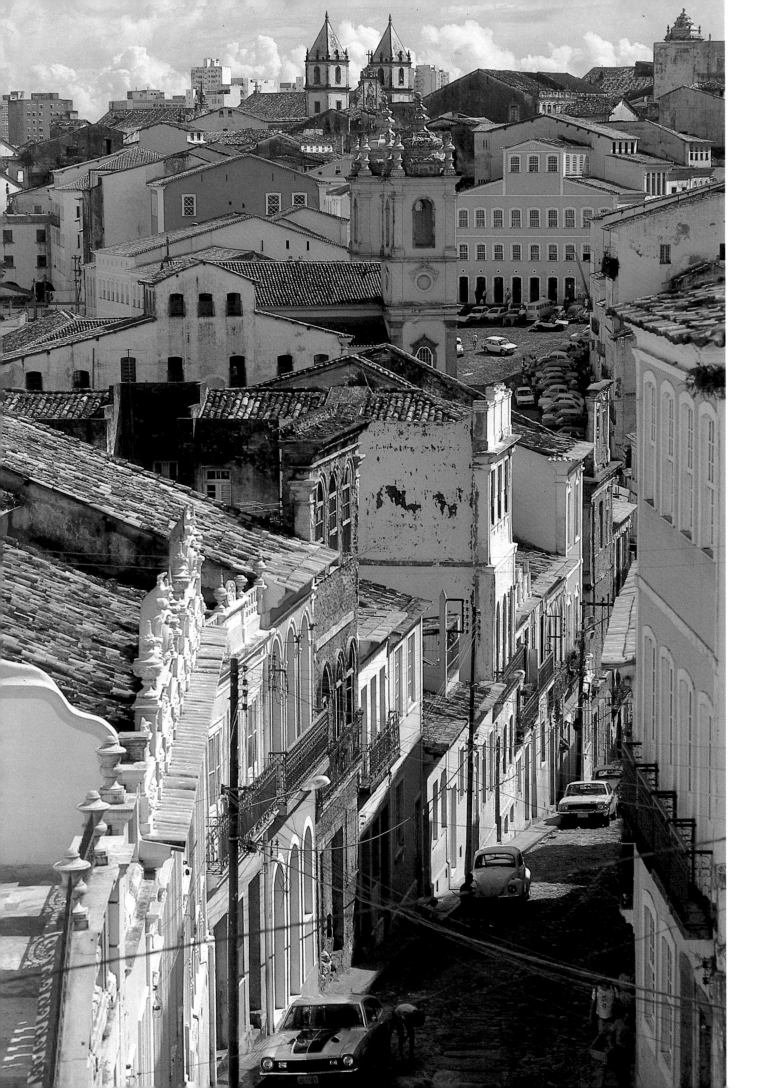

More than once I have written that Africa is our spiritual home. We are at least as much African as Iberian in our sensitiveness, our way of looking at life and the world, our manner of reacting to events, our way of living our own lives and sharing others, of thinking and acting. The contribution made by Africans to the formation of our national culture is of paramount importance. The vitality and strength of the Blacks was stronger than the whip or Holy water. The African spirit lived through the terrible conditions of slavery, keeping its originality but mixing over the course of time with the two other cultures to produce the singular mixed-race culture of the Bahians and Brazilians, perhaps unique in the world. Here everything is mixed together: the languages which were spoken in the houses of the masters, in the slaves' huts and in the forests; the saints imported from the Iberian peninsula, the *orishas* from Africa, the *iaras* and *cabocles* from the rivers and forests. Half-castes are we all, may the Lord of Bonfim and *Oshala* be praised, *amen, aché*!

And the beauty of Bahia is thereby increased, it

acquires its own character, its own indestructible mystery.

The city is on two levels. The Lower Town goes from the historical centre around the gulf, passing the Mont-Serrat Point with its small church of the beginning of the 17th century, then the sacred hill of Bonfim and, leaving behind the peninsula of Itapagipe, it continues towards the poor suburbs and the old railway line of the East Company. The Upper Town starts at the summit of the hill facing the port and follows aristocratic streets up and down the hills and valleys, nonchalantly paralleling the sinuous line of beaches all the way beyond the bay entry to the Atlantic itself. The inhabitants go up and down from one town to the other by means of the Lacerda lift (which is to Bahia what the Eiffel Tower is to Paris), by funiculars or by age-old ramps. Houses with common frontages descend by degrees to the foot of the verdant slope making you think of skyscrapers on their side. The bright blue and pink colours leap out of the luxuriant vegetation. Here the two halves meet. In Bahia nowhere can be separated from anywhere else. The stamp of Bahia comes from all around — a life of intensity.

In the street containing the multinational skyscraper, a street actor sets up the boards for his superb free show. He just needs a lizard or snake, a crocodile or a sloth, or simply a pack of cards, and he is off in front of his audience. His gift of the gab, his quips, his tricks quickly produce laughter and applause. He has imagination enough to be able to sell with ease the miracle cure which will cure all illnesses. Outside the government palace, the popular poet holds up his little

pamphlets by a piece of string. Without paying any taxes or key money, he sets up his walking library in the open air — a marvellous assortment of dramatic events, tragedy, the comical and the lyrical which faithfully translate the feelings of the people — their sanction and their protests.

The popular poet spouts his words to an ever-changing public which has no trouble assimilating the art since the metre is traditional and the musical rhythm well-known. At the market, installed in its beautiful building in the Lower Town, the tourist contemplates the richness of the local Bahian and Brazilian artisanat and the patient vendors sell them an introduction to Afro-Bahian culture and hang round the necks of the girls from São Paulo, New York or Tokyo necklaces in the colours of *Echou, Shango, Ogoun* and *Yansan*.

In front of the episcopal palace, on the Campo Grande square, things can suddenly happen as if by magic — a tambourine or *berimbao* or an *agogo* player or a couple of strapping lads who give an exhibition of *capoeira*, a way of fighting imported from Angola by the slaves which has become a ritual dance and game, merely simulating the mortal blows. A circle of spectators rapidly forms and passers-by quickly forget their work and their hurry. No one wants to miss such a wonderful show. Some Bolshoi dancers, stopping over in Bahia, gape open-mouthed and cannot understand how the participants in the *capoeira* can attain such an extraordinary precision with such grace and harmony in the succession of lunges and dodges, such a suppleness in the movements of the body, the slow sinuous gestures becoming fast as an arrow to give the coup de grace — all this through improvisation — no long years of tiresome, daily practice. On the beaches on the Atlantic coast, near to the big tourist hotels, the crowd on the beach sun-bathing, needs no invitation to join in the hauling in of the fishing net left the day before to catch *charéu*, the most popular local fish. About sixty fishermen gather around the chief and his two lieutenants, one in charge of manœuvres in the sea, the other for the shore. Placed beyond where the waves start to break, the net catches the shoals of fish as they pass. The following morning, divers go down from rafts to evaluate how much fish has been caught. If the catch is big enough, the order to pull it in goes out. The two lieutenants, one on the shore, one in the sea, send

signals between each other to control the manœuvre. When the fishermen are in place, swimming and holding on to the net, a song goes up marking the beginning of the long haul. On the beach, women and children, bathers and tourists get hold of the crude hemp rope and pull. They unite their voices to those coming from the sea, words which talk about the adundant fish. Or sometimes there are no words : the only sounds which come from throats lashed with salt-water are inarticulate, a sort of drawn-out wailing whose rhythm is governed by the breathing, by the movement of the feet as they dig in heavily into the sand and by the movement of the hands as they heave on the heavy net.

Over on the shores of the lake of Abaeté, a tiny pearl in the middle of the Itapoa dunes, a lagoon whose dark waters are set in the whiteness of the sand, the young girls of rich families lead the female tourists to a mysterious and purifying bathe. They pass the washerwomen carrying out their crude work on the banks. What grace of a black goddess there is in the languorous motion of this girl with blond hair. And what queen of the Old World has taught the brown washerwoman to carry her package of washing on her head with such style ? Only the virtues of the mixing of blood, of the symbiosis of cultures could make them so alike and so beautiful. Ah, Bahia the melting-pot : riches and poverty, drama and poetry.

A thick layer of religion submerges the town of Bahia. Faith is one of the clearest expressions of the humanism of the place. It is a faith felt and practised in a special but irrefutible manner. What would become of the men and women born here, the old man or the child, if, in

36

37

the moments of intense sadness or moments of sheer joy, they could not exclaim from the depths of their hearts : « God is greater ? » God is present everywhere in the town since the arrival of the first ships in the bay, since the disembarkment of Cabral at Porto Seguro where the first mass was said for the safe crossing and for the unhoped for discovery of such a huge and beautiful land. Apart from the Portuguese crew, this solemn ceremony had an audience equally unhoped for : that of a large group of indigenous natives who had come in their dug-outs. These made known the knowledge of the cross, the liturgical garments of the priest and the new god which had just arrived, a god which soon accepted to live, somewhat unwillingly it is true, alongside the pagan god of the natives, Tupan. And another god came to Bahia aboard the first Negro ship in the hearts of the Negroes confined in their filthy holds. This god had strange-sounding names : *Ogoum, Oshossi* and *Shango*. This time the god was not a penitent apostle but a hunter and warlord from the forests of Africa. This god too soon took the initiative by assimilating itself with the Catholic god.

Legend attributes to Bahia 365 Catholic churches, one for every day of the year. A song from Caymmi, well-known in all Brazil, confirms this exaggeration ;

    « In the first, I was baptised

    In the second, I was confirmed

    In the third, I will be married

    To the woman I love. »

In Bahia, the houses of the gods are so many and so beautiful, some so sumptuous, that there is not an unbeliever who is not touched. Almost all the churches   **40** are grandiose with their imposing towers and Baroque or Renaissance facades or sometimes with all kinds of styles mixed up together. In the magnificent interiors, precious wood sculptures are painted with gold, ceilings are covered with ancient paintings and the high parts of the walls are decorated with precious panels of *azulejos*. On bended knee before the marvellous statues of the saints painted by the first anonymous artists of the area, the Bahians confess their sins and repent their numerous faults. They make vows so that their requests should be granted and offer religiously an ex-voto either painted on wood, or sculptured in wood or modelled in wax. The poorest among them will leave an offering in his favourite church of a simple photograph of himself in his sailor's clothes taken straight after escaping a shipwreck say, or a clump of the hair of his child who has survived a serious fever. God is all over Bahia. His presence is felt equally through the bells of the inumerable churches in the most picturesque parts of the town as in the small chapels of the poorest quarters. The faith of the Bahians is spread generously over the whole and the strength of their belief is such that the number of places of worship seems to be multiplied to such an extent that it confers on the faded colours a seriousness which cannot be contradicted.

Educated people, perhaps not necessarily firm believers, put the number of Catholic churches in Bahia at 76. But one must also take into consideration the 600-odd places of worship of the Candomblé cult — the different Afro-Bahian sects. These *terreiros*, the sanctuaries of the Negro religion, were rigorously banned up

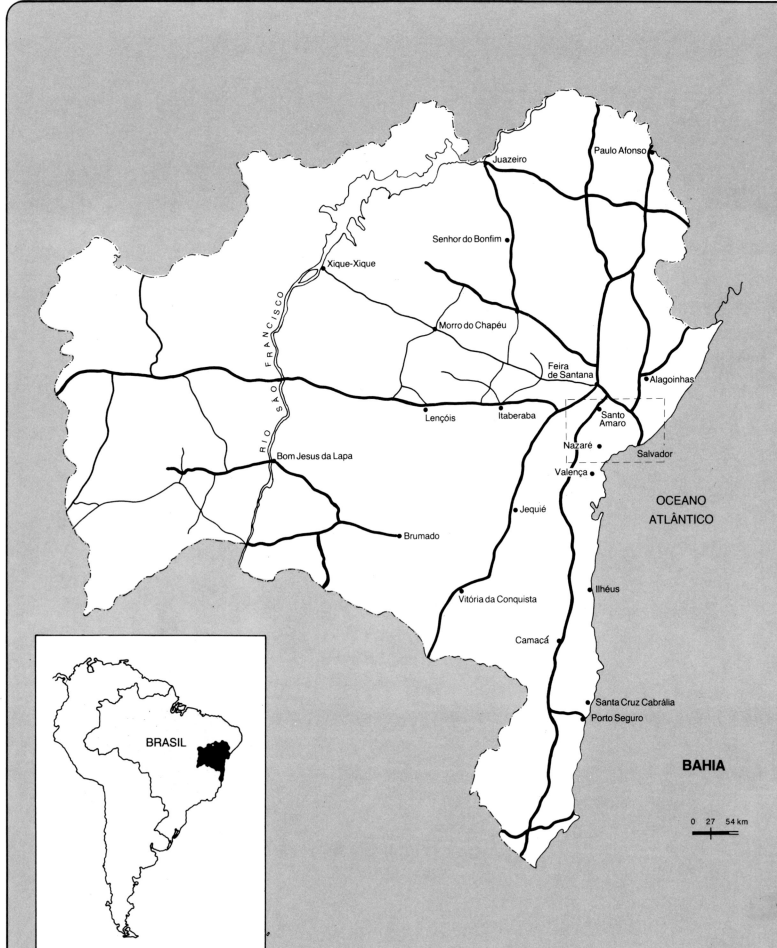

Juazeiro

Paulo Afonso

Senhor do Bonfim

Xique-Xique

RIO SÃO FRANCISCO

Morro do Chapéu

Feira de Santana

Alagoinhas

Lençóis

Itaberaba

Santo Amaro

Nazaré

Salvador

Bom Jesus da Lapa

Valença

OCEANO ATLÂNTICO

Jequié

Brumado

Ilhéus

Vitória da Conquista

Camacá

Santa Cruz Cabrália

Porto Seguro

BAHIA

BRASIL

0   27   54 km

44

Brazil is the largest country in South America with about 8.5 million square kilometres and 120 million habitants. The state of Bahia, with 560.000 square kilometres and 9.5 million inhabitants is situated in the north-east with a long Atlantic coastline. The Bahian Recôncavo traditionally supply cocoa, sisal, tobacco, coffee and hides and recently oil products.

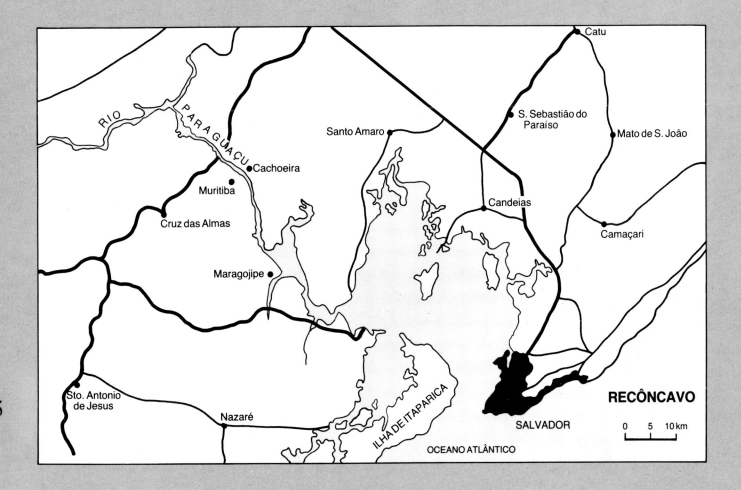

until the 1940s and the sects were persecuted by the police who arrested the *babalorishas* (priests) and the *yawos* (daughters of the gods). Since the days of colonisation, the members of the sect used houses lost in the vegetation on the outskirts of the town. But the strength of this popular culture has overcome hostility. Today, the sects are legally registered and membership of these cults is no longer proscribed by law. In fact, they have become important tourist attractions. And because the town has seen considerable expansion due to the installation of industries, the *terreiros* now find themselves in the middle of the city. The major factor in this victory was the recourse by the Catholic Church to cohabitation with the cults. This led to saints and *orishas* being present together on altars in homes ; later the church ceremonies themselves displayed an aspect of fetishism each time the people took part. Almost as old as the churches themselves, the *terreiros* gained another important victory when one of the oldest — the Casa Branca which is 350 years old — was listed by the national body devoted to the preservation of the memory of the people, a decision which would have been unthinkable two decades ago.

PEOPLE

MERRY MAKING

With nightfall, when the *atabaques* (ritual drums) start to sound, the Bahian joins in the ceremonies to the African gods, acquitting himself of his obligations to them, offering food to them and sacrificing animals in their honour. He asks the high priestess for an *ebö*, an offering to vanquish the disappointments of life and love. One can see *ebös* all the time at the junctions of tracks and even on surfaced roads, in the suburbs and in the centre. No Bahian will approach these little packets containing flour and oil or old copper money or candles or a strangled black chicken. Drivers go round them carefully in their cars — better not to take any risks.

A faith for all moments, for all the gods, but without dogma, without limitations or exclusivity. A deep

59

feeling but diffused, bringing together the gods of men and stirring them into his daily life. A catholicism which includes anticlericism because if, here, the divinity is the object of the most fervent veneration, his representative has no place in this glory. But the priests of Candomblé are members of the family of gods and are regarded as intimates of the *orishas* themselves. The pure Negro, attached to his African roots, does not exist : for the Bahian, Africa is like any other unknown country with which one can have relations which do not imply subordination to an imperialism. If the Catholic Church looks for a way to cohabit with socialism, the Bahian pays no heed. Nor is he any more worried when he sees the *Candomblé* begin to convert to *Umbanda*, the majority religion today in the urban population of Brazil. He has his faith, a faith embedded in his capacity to live even in today's difficult circumstances. And if you ask him in a dubious tone of voice if he will be able to persuade an alluring but stubborn brown girl on to the beach or into bed, he replies with a profound religious conviction, « I have faith ! » His faith is without limits, his gods are many and benevolent. And they are half-caste too, as many as they are. In this city, the popular culture is so powerful with such a rich tradition and such strong roots, that it conditions all artistic or literary creativity. In Bahia, the popular culture penetrates the senses and determines the national character of the arts. The popular inspiration is present even in the most intellectually subtle work of art.

How could it be otherwise when the town itself is the most beautiful sculpture one could ask to behold ? How could the artist trained in an academy but a native of Bahia not follow this creative vein which he carries in his blood since the cradle, mixed in his blood for centuries ? This popular culture fed his childhood and is with him day and night wherever he may be in this city so animated ans sparkling.

All the arts — drawing, engraving, painting, sculpture, poetry, prose, theatre, music, dance, singing, etc — are practised every day in Bahia by the popular artists who work in a way which goes from total dilettantism to the most absolute professionalism. Poets write their verses, print them and sell them themselves. The covers of their pamphlets are decorated with popular engravings, these too derived from the common imagination and a tried technique. In the workshops of Pelourinho or Tabuão, two of the most intensely lively but wretched quarters, the « miracle » specialists creat exvotos painted on wood or canvas, sculpted out of wood or modelled in wax, all with great cleverness. From their hands also come the statues of the saints which decorate the corners of homes. They have no need of boutiques to show their creations which cannot be seen in art galleries or museums unless they have been « discovered » by clever « merchants ». Certain among them attain a national notoriety. Their clientele and their profits often pass those of their learned colleagues. Song and dance are practised in the streets and in the squares which are always in carnival. Brazil and a good part of the world sings with the voice of Bahia since it was here that the samba was born. Tourists are delighted to see folklore groups interpret for them the *macoulélé*, the *samba de roda*, the hymns of

invocation to the *orishas*, all African in origin, but also the songs of *Sertão* and the high plateaus of Diamantina from the Portuguese Middle Ages, sad languid airs which tell of the goat-herds of the mountains and the arid plains on the banks of the São Francisco river. The *capoeira* and the danses of the *Candomblé* are ballets of extraordinary beauty which achieve the greatest success on whatever stage they are played without the need to recompose them or make them understandable since they are so already. They give an artistic form to an anonymous creation and reproduce it without ever misinterpreting.

Today they make up an integral part of world cinema as seen in the films of Glauber Rocha — extracts of the saga of *Sertão* of Bahia. Carybé, a Brazilian born by chance in Buenos Aires, but the most Bahian of all painters, has a world reputation ; the black Brazilian sculptor Agnaldo de Jésus, who died when he was thirty, won the Grand Prix of the Negro Art Festival of Nigeria ; and the samba of Dorival Caymmi conquered Brazil and has travelled to China, the Soviet Union, Japan and the United States. The values of the cross-bred culture of Bahia are at the same time unique and universal.

The Bahians, being believers, venerating all the gods and born artists, need a consistent diet. The culinary art is another trait which marks the popular culture of Bahia and is one of its greatest charms. With the Negro ships came palm oil and pimento, the ritual foods of the Negroes and the preferred delicacies of the *orishas*. On the river banks grew coconut trees and the Portuguese brought their recipes for sweets, adding sugar to the

66

cook milk. The flavours were also mixed : manioc with indigenous corn, white flour, and infinite number of dishes based on corn, palm oil, coco milk, peanut and ginger. The Portuguese dishes took on a spicy taste, more pronounced and stronger. The preparations for cooking lost their aggressivity in exchange for a delicacy which they had never possessed before. To this mix, the rudimentary Indian cooking added leaves, roots and the flesh of game. This then constituted the Bahian cooking, unquestionably and without exaggeration one of the most refined and succulent in the world. In the long list of Bahian specialities are dishes like *moqueca de siri mole, vatapá* and *efó* which would figure proudly in any very selective encyclopedia of world cuisine.

In any restaurant, whether it be modest or sumptuous, in a four-star hotel or from a street stall, in a lorry-driver's stop on the outskirts of town or in the streets of the financial centre, even in the poorest quarters, the dishes served would befit a palace. From Rio to São Paolo, from the extreme south to the central plateaus, people come to taste the small fritters made

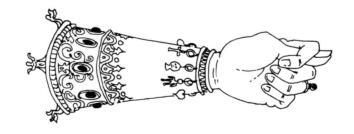

from the paste of a certain type of bean which is cooked before you in boiling palm oil : acarajé. People come from miles around simply to savour this acarajé of Bahia including the distinguished and highly-educated. Come to Bahia, it is waiting for you. If you love your own city, whether it be Rio, Paris, London, Leningrad, Venice of the canals, Prague of the old towers, Pekin or Vienna, you should make a trip to Bahia because a new love will take over your heart. A splendid town, married to the sea, holder of mystery and beauty. This is the sea where Yemanjá lives, the goddess with five names. The gloomy call of the *atabaques* fills the night which envelops the mansions beneath the moon, the churches of gold and the sides of the hills charged with so much history.

The town will hold you enthralled in its magic charm and you will give it your heart as never before ; you will never forget Bahia, its immense beauty will get under your skin and its enchanted universe will excite you forever.

This is my city. In any town that I have been to, I have found in it such and such an aspect of beauty. But nowhere else is it so apparent and nowhere does one feel so happy. It is here that I want to die when my time comes, feeling the breeze which comes from the sea, listening to the drums of the *atabaque* at night and the singing of the fishermen. In this town of Bahia, set on the hill, impregnated by the sea.

Bahia is always celebrating, visitors say, surprised by the succession of festivities which fill the year from January to December almost without interruption. The roads, the squares, even the sea are filled with the joy of

71

life. The festivities are many in number, some very old and traditional, others which appeared more recently. Whether they be linked to the Catholic religion or the Afro-Bahian sects, whether they be civic commemorations or a carnival, they have one thing in common : their simplicity and their open character. These festivals have no fancy trappings — their greatest attraction is the people themselves. This is where the fascination comes from whether you see it every day or if it is for the first time. The festivals have such a human warmth that they seem to have cast a spell. Tourists tell curious journalists that by taking part they find out more about themselves, they discover their own personality, their identity and they feel an impression of freedom.

Where does this magic spell come from, how can we explain it ? The Bahian festivals give to the people the streets and squares so that they can celebrate, peacefully and democratically together, the rites of courtesy and kindness. Everyone is welcome. The rules of dress and behaviour are swept aside. With no other excuse than that of tradition, people get together and fraternise. They eat and drink, dance and sing, with no other aim than that of being together. It is impossible not to feel this special atmosphere and impossible to resist its contagious attraction. Here then, in all its simplicity, is the biggest mystery of Bahia.

These festivals, of which some have been held regularly for centuries, have a very particular meaning : people are stronger than oppression and mysery. Life is sometimes so difficult and cruel that it seems unbearable. But the people resist, they do not give up. They make merry, they dance, sing and burst into laughter :

they are never beaten.

The Procession of the Lord of Navigators.

In the Bahian festival cycle, the procession of the good lord of navigators is the most important of the maritime festivals, and where the Catholic fervour is the most intense. Celebrated on the 1st January, it brings in the New Year. In fact it starts the day before with the carrying of the sacred statue from the beautiful church in the quarter of Boa Viagem — where panels in *azulejos* tell of miracles during shipwrecks and of ships saved from a watery grave — to the church of the Conceição da Praia in the centre of the town. Here the statue is received by that of Notre Dame de la

Conception and the faithful venerate the visitor saint. The next day, the great procession takes place which in itself is worth a trip to Bahia. A dressed galeon — the same one has been used for two centuries — carries the sacred statue. Hundreds of boats of all kinds gather on the sea to form the procession and bring it to its glory. The cortege makes its way towards the mouth of the bay so that the Lord Jesus can bless the ocean. From there the procession returns to Boa Viagem where the statue is put back in its place in the church with all the marks of veneration which are due to it.

During the whole procession, on all the small craft, the crowd sings and dances — religious canticals and popular sambas are all mixed together. The most common form of dress is the bikini. The Catholic character of the festival does not exclude religious cohabitation : behind the large cloak of the Saviour of Navigators is placed the abébé (fan) of Janaina, the goddess of the sea.

The Festival of Kings and the Washing of the Church of Bonfim.

The journey of the Magi kings in search of the crib of Jesus was the inspiration for the Festival of Kings which takes place on the 6th January. On this occasion, groups of boys and girls run along the streets singing carols and dancing the *bumba-meu-boi*. Some of their costumes are hundreds of years old and the parade, lit by their lanterns, lights up the whole of Bahia. This festival, which is one of the oldest, is stamped by its tenderness and draws a large popular participation. On the morning of the third Thursday of January, one of the biggest Bahian festivals takes place : the washing of the church of Bonfim, the culmination of a celebration which in fact last for an entire week. On the Saturday and Sunday, singers and dancers parade mixing carnival and the Festival of Kings ; on the Monday of the Ribeira with its street stalls, the people eat and drink while the samba happens in the street. But the washing of the church of the most popular saint of the town is the great event for which a holiday is declared. The procession leaves the Church of the Conceição da Praia forming an enormous cortege. A harmonious confusion reigns in the canticals, with the Catholic repertory in butchered Latin mixing with the songs of the Macumba in Yorouba. The faithful who know neither sing sambas and popular marches accompanied by guitars, *cuicas* and tambourines. The saint looks on favourably at all these manifestations in his honour. During this very special Thursday, no sins are committed in the streets of Bahia.

The « daughters of the saint » of Candomblé make up part of the cortege. They wear blouses and starched white skirts covered with flowers. Marching in the crowd, they carry on their heads, miraculously steady, jugs, jars and vases painted with the glaze of Maragogipe — a town in Recôncavo — and covered with pretty drawings. They will offer to the saint, the purest objects in the world : water and flowers, and joy too. Following the women comes a procession of children, sweet sellers, who on this day have their arms full of aromatic branches. With the women in their local costume, they form the guard of honour for the Lord of Bonfim. Next in the cortege are the water-carriers pulling their small carts and pushing their donkeys.

The carts are hidden under the flowers and the animals are scarcely visible beneath multicoloured pieces of paper, giving them a fabulous aspect. White dominates in the costumes, a hommage to Oshaloufan, the oldest orisha of Candomblé, assimilated with the Catholic saint. Summer fruits — mangoes, pineapples, oranges seem to jump out of the overloaded platters. They are for the saint of Bonfim, who, like all the orishas, accepts fruit as an offering during his festival in Bahia.

In the square at the top of the hill, in front of the church, little stalls are decorated with paper banners made gay by the colours of typical dishes: the gold yellow of the

vatapa, the green of the *carourou*, the black of the *efó* — mixed up with a profusion of multi-coloured foods and drinks. The choir starts the samba which begins the washing. The square is packed. People climb trees to get a view of the spectacle. Women, children and officials are all mixed up together in front of the temple. The women splash out the water from the jars while others begin to wash the square. It is the water of Oshala which flows in hommage to the Catholic saint. The turbans of the Bahians move in rhythm to the washing of the church. It is a magnificent ballet performed to the sound of Negro chants, an immense *macumba* — a fetishist ceremony performed at a Catholic temple.

The festival finishes during the night of Sunday. Up until the end, the crowd sings and dances, eats and drinks, giving themselves up to the celebration in the uproar and the jollity.

In the early morning, the crowd moves over to the neighbouring quarter of Ribeira where the samba continues as if to anticipate the upcoming carnival. On the 2nd February is the festival on the ocean. In the folklore of long ago, a colony of fishermen from Rio Vermelho, then a tiny village outside the town with nothing in common with today's suburb, lived through a strange and frightening event. Pulling up their net set to catch caranx — the basic fish diet of the poor people — they saw among the fish and crabs the siren Yemanjá herself — the goddess of the sea, she who the Indians saw in their rivers and which the black slaves brought from Africa and incorporated in the Bahian culture. She had the face and breasts of a woman with a beauty without equal, and a tail of silver scales : Yemanjá seemed to have lost consciousness or have been plunged into a deep sleep characteristic of the orishas. Marvelling, the fishermen and their wives took up the inert body of Janaina and carried it to the only sacred spot in the village : the tiny chapel of Sainte Anne, built for them by the Catholic priests, sparkling white in the centre of the sandy square. Men, women and children gathered around their orisha and, in order to wake her, intoned their native incantations. The « daughters of the gods » who were consecrated to her executed their wild dances and the sound of drums filled the night. The fairytale night over, Yemanjá awoke and rested under the portal of Sainte Anne, just below the multi-coloured wood statue of the saint.

The fishermen were delighted to see Ynaê among them but they were to have a new fright when they saw the apparition of the vicar of the parish, awakened too by

the ceremony. The priest was no less stunned than the fishermen. Although his church had undoubtedly been profaned by the pagan ceremony, he had to believe the evidence of his amazed eyes. It was clearly Yemanjá who was on the altar of Sainte Anne but the white saint did not appear to be affected. She remained serene and smiling in her coloured, wood statue. The priest overcame his fear and his prejudices and coming up to Janaina, he touched the tail still wet from the sea. Then, silent and unmoving, he stayed there looking at her. Such a beauty could only be divine. The dawn light announced the coming of day and the priest came out of his stupor, asking that Yemanjá be removed from there. But since this priest was a young half-caste native from the village, he did not issue a condemning sermon or use violent words. Instead he formulated his request with humility. He watched the fishermen leave the church with the orisha who dived into the waters, taking the strongest and most handsome fisherman with her.

And because these facts have been handed down and the memory of such an important event has never died, the people of Bahia come together at Rio Vermelho on the 2nd February for the great festival of Yemanjá.

On the square of Sainte Anne, where the chapel of the legend still exists, the *Yawos* of Janaina start to arrive after dawn, dressed in their ritual costumes and jewellery. Each one brings an offering and leaves it in the « weighing house ».

In this small building where the sales of the daily catches take place, can also be found the *pégi* of Janaina, the altar of the orisha. It is why it is topped by

90

the effigy of a siren in metal. The offerings are cuttings of tissue or boxes of soap or rice, hair-clips, ribbons, rings, flacons of perfume, braded slippers or earings — all sorts of objects for women because Janaina is vain. The fishermen's wives, fearing for the safety of their men, write letters to Yemanjá asking for protection and asking her for calm seas and abundant fish. They try to get into the good graces of Janaina so that she does not turn her desirous eyes on their husbands. They know that Janaina chooses among their men her lover, the man she will leave with without warning at the festival of love, at the celebration of the shipwreck. Bouquet after bouquet of flowers are carried to the *pégi*. The gardens of the town, rich or poor, are pillaged so that on this day, all the flowers should be offered to Yemanjá. In the square, carnival troups get caught up with groups improvising music. The festival is extraordinarily joyful. On the *pégi* of the siren, an enormous fish in wood receives the offerings of the fishermen.

Hundreds of other offerings fill great wicker-baskets — some expensive but for the most part cheap souvenirs, because the people are poor, very poor. The queue of people bringing presents extends in front of the weighing house all morning while everybody sings and dances on the square.

Towards the middle of the afternoon, the offerings are put into a cortege led by the « Mothers » and « Daughters » of the Saint before being transferred to a fishing boat.

This boat takes the head of a procession of small and large craft which leaves to the acclamations of the crowd filling the square and lining the bank. The boats

go a long way out from the coast to the place where Yemanjá is, surrounded by fish and clad in seaweed and shellfish. They form a circle around her and the offerings are thrown. Men and women await the decision of Janaina. On the banks too the crowd waits expectantly : will Yemanjá accept the offerings of her sons. If she does and takes them with her to the deep, the year will be a good one for fishing and navigating. If, on the other hand, she rejects them and leaves them floating on the surface, that signifies that the orisha has left for the country of Aioka, that she is angry with the fishermen and they will have storms, deaths and a dearth of fish ; and for the women, funerals. But, suddenly, a clamour goes up from the boats as the « Mothers of the Saint » strike up the song of joy. Janaina receives the offerings into her green hair, into her coral arms and on her foaming breasts. Acclamations go up from the bank and the dancing starts up again, the *samba* and the *capoeira*, helped on by the instruments of the poor people. The boats come back on shore and the celebrations go on the whole week until Sunday when it becomes the feast of Saint Anne, the Catholic saint, saluted with the same joy and by the same people with fervour and gaiety.

THE RECÔNCAVO

The town of Bahia, theatre of a permanent fête, and such intense day-to-day life, is encircled by the string of small towns of Recôncavo, a complete contrast with Bahia. As if they were a ring which is prevented by the ocean from completely forming, they surround the capital with a nostalgic atmosphere of a life which has stopped in time, a remote, forgotten time. This region was the first in Brazil to be colonised by the Portuguese discoverers. When the virgin forest was chopped down to take out the precious wood including the Brazil wood from which the country takes its name, the black earth which was left was covered with sugar cane and tobacco. Out of sight of Bahia, a soft and attractive countryside unfolded. Plantation houses were built near running water or on the sea at the bottom of All

Saints Bay. These habitations were the tributaries to the port exporting products such as sugar, eau-de-vie, rolled tobacco, the first cigars, all products which were avidly absorbed by the European market. Africa took the almost unusable scraps from the tobacco production and exchanged them for a merchandise of even less value : men and women of black race captured in the heart of the forests, taken from their tribes and, heavy in chains, put into the foul holds of the slave ships to make up the unpaid workforce which developed the feudal economy of Recôncavo. These blacks were robbed on two counts : they lost their individual liberty but also the possibility of living according to their culture. A Bahian poet summed up this abominable crime in a few lines :

First
They took me away from Africa
And then
They took Africa away from me.

The plantation settlements, living in isolated self-sufficiency in the country and in non-stop production thanks to the sweat and blood of the slaves, formed a feudal and mediaeval society. The lords of the land, installed in their imposing mansions, reigned over the slave masses with an unlimited power over life and death, under the protective wing of the Church which constructed here some of the most beautiful temples in Brazil. Having been given the land by Lisbon, these lords mimicked the manners and behaviour of courtiers. Through the Crown they added to their common names the noble titles of count, baron or marquis. The rapid development of agriculture and the production of

122

sugar and tobacco provoked the creation of towns which grew fast and became important : Cachoeira, São Felix, Muritiba, Cruz das Almas, Santo António de Jesus, Maragogipe, São Francisco do Conde and some twenty others. The reign of the sugar barons lasted until the end of the 18th century. The discovery of gold in Minas Gerais and the transfer of the capital to Rio de Janeiro displaced the economic axis of the colony. Bahia was condemned to isolation, losing its riches and its prestige. The decline of sugar cane and tobacco and the fall in the price of these products on the export markets paralysed the Recôncavo. The technological backwardness and feudal system threatened the survival of the agriculture in the absence of alternative proposals.

The honorary titles were classified in the family archives generation after generation and these pretty towns of the Recôncavo went into a deep slumber which was to last two centuries. The areas of dark green for tobacco and the lighter green for sugar cane gradually became fewer. The primitive cigar manufacturers went out of business as did the only cigarette manufacturer in the area. The only thing to remain was an artisanal production of cigars for local consumption. In a sense the towns had won — isolated, stagnating, they had been able to keep their characteristic beauty within the marvellous countryside. When the wind makes the white plumes of the sugar canes ripple, the countryside is magnificent — its beauty can only be compared to that of fields of wheat. The ruins of the plantation buildings and the age-old factories, together with the lords' mansions and the Catholic chapels

appear in this splendour like ghosts from the past. Cachoeira and São Felix, twin cities on opposite banks of the river Paraguaçu, are the best example of what one can see in the Recôncavo. From Salvador, it is less than two hours to get there either by car or by boat up the river. The best way is by *saveiro*, the sail-boat typical to Bahia : first one crosses the bay, then up the Paraguaçu with its banks planted with cane, tobacco and palm oil trees. After Cachoeira, a road climbs for a few kilometres towards the mountain in the direction of Muritiba. From whatever point on this route, the view over the valley is magnificent.

In the colonial towns, today protected by the state as part of the national heritage, everything is worth seeing : the streets where the big mansions are with their balconies sculptured in wood, the imposing but harmonious mass of the old convents, the commercial buildings of the river port. Everywhere is deserted, empty, still. It is the excitement of life which gives the municipal market its animation. This is where all the sale of foodstuffs and the savoury fruits of the region takes place. The people gossip with their comrades from neighbouring plantations. It is also the place where the local artisanat is on display : objects in clay, straw, wood and metal.

But the big event in this field does not take place in Cachoeira but at Nazaré das Farinhas, another agglomeration of the Recôncavo. Here is held every year the pottery fair, which has an important place on the tourist calendar of Bahia. All sorts of ceramic products from many towns in the region are to be found all along the streets and in the squares. One cannot help but admire the imagination and cleverness of the people in conserving but evolving the traditional forms from which they draw their inspiration.

Today, the Recôncavo is beginning to awake from its lethargy. Oil wells have recently been exploited although this is on the decline. But hydroelectric plants on the river São Francisco produce electricity and highways linking the north and the south of the country have been built. These are new and efficient stimulants to the economy. The sugar and tobacco industries are taking off again giving optimism to the population of Recôncavo. The production of alcohol which is replacing petrol in engines and particularly car engines is also becoming important. The sleepy towns are waking up again and hope relives. But town and country are keeping their traditional aspect and enchant the visitor with their gentle beauty and quietness.

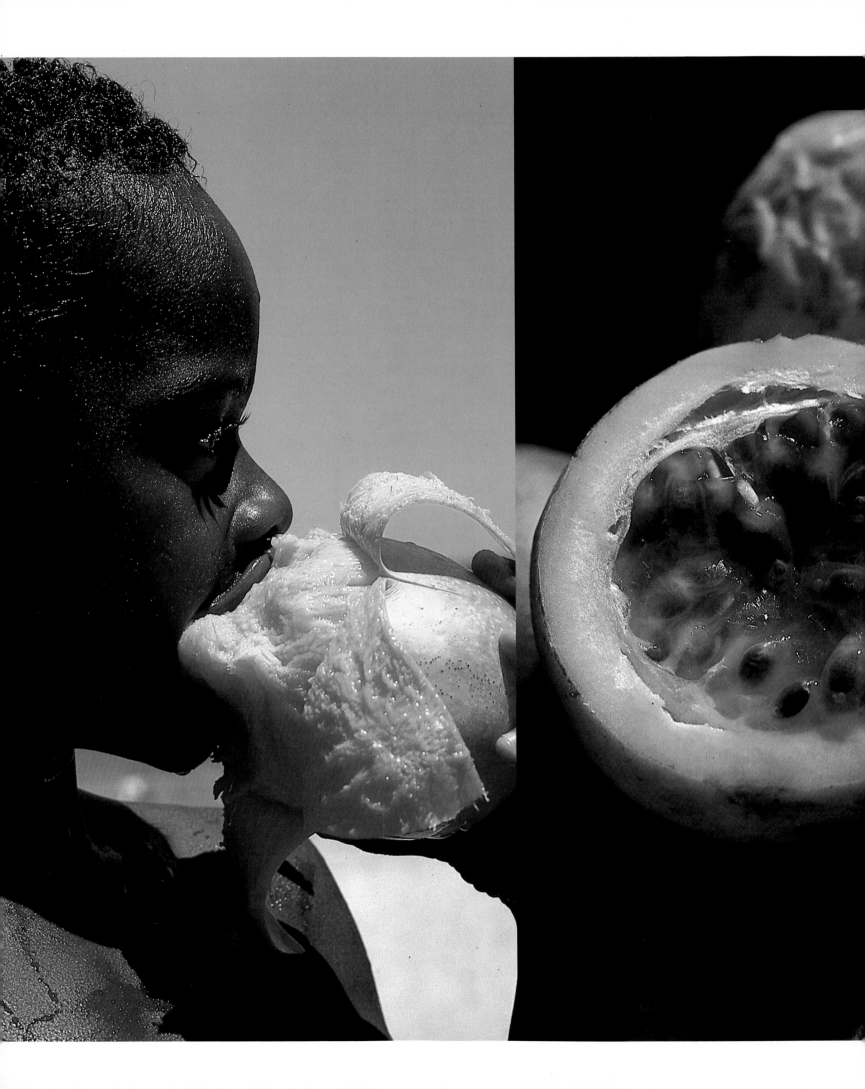

THREE REGIONS OF THE STATE OF BAHIA

The state of Bahia is only just now going through its stage of development given its basically agrarian economy based on semi-feudal practices which adapt difficulty to industrialisation. It is a territory as large as France where the latifundium and monocultures cover vast areas. The rural population vegetates in semi-human conditions waiting for a progress which has only just started and which hardly improves their lot. The south of the state is given over to the monoculture of cocoa production. This takes up a vast region and spreads into the state of Espirito Santó. As an export product with a high return on investment, it produces fortunes and has left its distinctive mark on the region. While the major part of the production is concentrated in the hands of a small number of planters and

companies, the small holdings play a dominant role too. The feudal system which exists in other regions of the state has given way to a capitalism which has transformed the peasant without land into a common worker. Either a native of the region or an emigré of *Sertao*, he has broken with the agricultural tradition he inherited — the vital joy of planting and harvesting what one has sown. He harvests and dries the cocoa of the owner and receives each week his measly wage to buy food from the market, food which he would in other times have produced with his own hands. The dream of possessing his own land, the dream of every field worker, has changed into a desire to find a better life in São Paulo.

Access to this region is easy by plane and by made-up roads which serve the towns, vibrant from the riches of the region. The people are proud of their tradition of fierce fights to conquer the land, with a body of legends which forms a literature and poetry which contributes substantially to the cultural panorama of the country. Being a native of the region myself, a good part of my work as an author relates to this hard reality. An invitation to visit the cocoa country should not be turned down. The towns there have their own special character strongly marked by an extraordinary dynamism, a wish to go forward and an abundance of riches which increase its beauty. The sea ports such as Ilhéus are particularly attractive despite the hot, humid climate. Itabuna, Ubaitaba, Guandu and some twenty other towns exercise a fascination which is linked to their dynamic economies. On the Atlantic coast are plantations of coconut palms which seem to be interminable and the cultivation of piassava palms whose oil has a host of industrial applications. They enhance the beauty of the beaches and certain historic sites such as Porto Seguro, Santa Cruz, Cabrália and Nova Viçosa where the first Portuguese ships landed. There is the national park protected by federal laws, exposed as it is to the menace of indiscriminate tourism against which the local population react. Close by is what is left of the indigenous native Indian tribes of Bahia who were subjected to rapacity and violent genocide.

The southwest of the state presents a completely different picture. While it is linked with Recôncavo by the same tradition of lost riches, and by the same air of abandonment, it is different for all that. This is the land of the plateau of Chapada Diamantina with a cold and dry climate. Its history keeps the memory of a far-gone time when for a short time it achieved a stature due to the extraction of precious stones. The mines threw up towns and caused a tumultuous flux of life bringing with it violence. Mucugê, Andarai, Rio de Contas, Livramento and above all Lençóis — veritable museum of the architecture and lifestyle of the colonial period — are impressively beautiful. For a long time they stagnated after the mines had run out, giving themselves over to cattle-raising. Recently, however, this region has been revitalised by the cultivation of coffee which has rapidly covered the countryside since the growing conditions are better than in the states of São Paulo or Paraná. The Chapada Diamantina has discovered again its destiny to be a rich zone and a new courage animates the population. Towns already more

than 200 years old are in the throws of development. The *Sertão* is a world of dreams and legends and sadness. The vegetation of the caatinga is stunted and hardly covers the bare earth which is cracked by the implacable sun. The dryness is a punishment from God, the people of *Sertão* say. In spite of everything, the people adapt themselves and in their leather garments, they drive their bovines and goats across the vast plains. Great irony : these plains are crossed by one of the largest rivers in the world, the São Francisco. It rises in Minas and flows for thousands of kilometres across the states of Bahia and Sergipe before going into the Atlantic at the confines of Alagoas. This great river is mother and father to the inhabitant of *Sertão*. It provides delicious fish and is the only sure way of travelling to the towns along its banks. It is the link between the plantations and the markets of the capital which can be reached by the old trains of the East Brazil network and now by two asphalt highways. But this river is also a punishment from God and not just because it does nothing in the fight against the drought. Its periodical floods wipe out feeble cultures and the inhabitants of the banks, leaving behind epidemics and death. The hydroelectric dams which bar the river's flow are scarcely of use to the inhabitants of this region but they are a promise of future progress and bring hope.

The *Sertão* have a rich catalogue of legends, of sagas of violence of the masters of the land, of the rich, all-powerful owners, and also of the stupifying miracles due to the clemency of the Good Jesus de Lapa. Situated on the banks of the river, the sanctuary of 162

Lapa attracts tens of thousands of pilgrims and also hords of fanatics who even today roam these regions forgotten by God and the Devil. The latter manifests himself however in the bands of *cangaceiros* which spread terror throughout the whole of the north-east. And he undoubtedly went among the warriors of Antonio Conselheiro, who commanded an army of fanatic pilgrims which routed government troops and fought bravely until they were exterminated in a war without mercy.

In the *Sertão*, of today, modern technology is being applied in a number of agro-industrial projects with promising results. But the inhabitants are not benefitting directly. They remain the poor raisers of scattered cattle without any other aid but their capacity to resist the droughts or floods and the hope that they will be saved by a hypothetical god to whom they hold out their hands.

The journey down the São Francisco is well worth the trouble — from Petrolina in Minas Gerais to Juazeiro in Bahia. One should come down the river slowly on board the flat-bottomed boats called *gaiolas* and admire the spectacle of the towns and riverside villages rich with local crafts. The trip takes six days and reveals a strange world, so absurd that it appears unreal, but of an undescribable beauty.

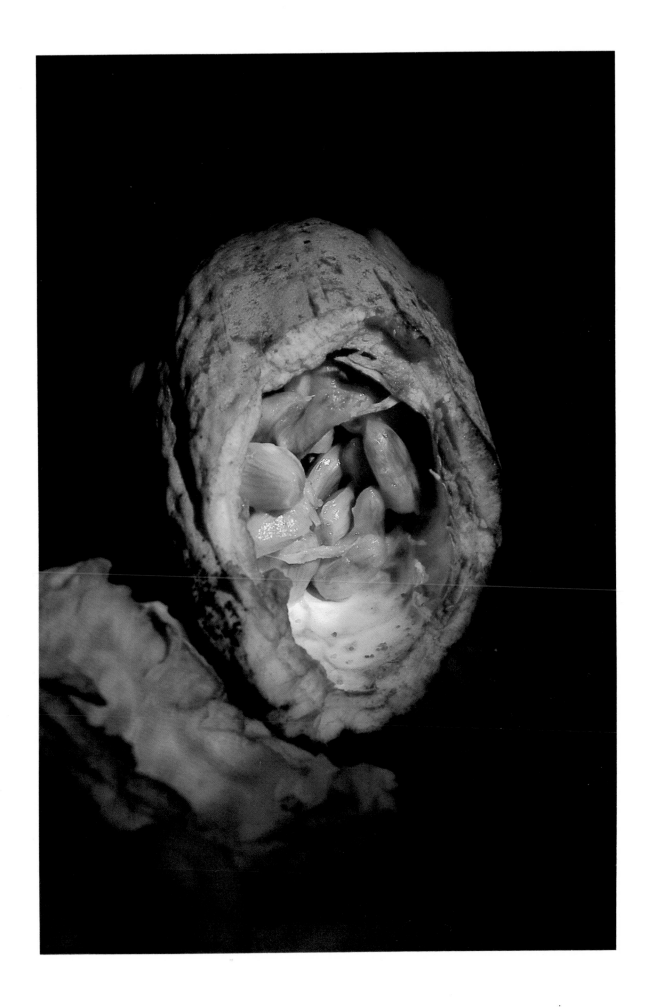

26 Bahia : from the top of the Luis Viana street one can see the Pelourinho square
27 The Rampa do Mercado

SALVADOR DA BAHIA

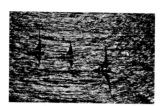

6-7 After a long day fishing, three « vela de pena » come back to port

30-31 Bahia : one of the most fascinating places in the world ; here the old port and the upper town

10-11 Morro de São Paulo has ravishingly beautiful beaches of white sand and this dream island, one hour from Valença.

34 The streets of the upper town are lined with houses with frontages in the classical, colonial style

14 A banana seller at the market
15 Rio Vermelho : gossipping on the quai of the port

38-39 Half dance, half fight, the **Capoeira** takes place in the squares to the delight of the tourists

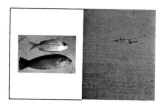

18-19 At five o'clock in the morning the fishermen set their nets to catch these colourful « salmonettes »

42 Behind the Museum of Sacred Art, a tiny street with couloured façades
43 Romance in action

22-23 This old fisherman smiles about his net full of « petetinguas »

46-47 The cross of St. Francis and the church of the « Ordem Terceira de Sao Domingos »

49 Our Lady of the Conception with the Royal Crown of D. Joao IV — Museum of Sacred Art, 17th century.

PEOPLE MERRY-MAKING

50-51 The Adoration of the Pastors — gilted wood coming from the chapel of São José de Antiga Sé, 1686, Museum of Sacred Art

60-61 On the third Thursday of January, the whole town of Bahia forms a procession to the church of Bonfim

52 Our Lord of the Cold Stone, attributed to Manoel Inacio da Costa, second half of the 18th century, Museum of Sacred Art
53 Convent of Carmes

64-65 The procession of the washing of Bonfim leaves the church of Conceicão da Praia in an harmonious confusion of music and songs

54-55 These touching ex-votos are framing a photograph of the Museum of Miracles at the Church of Bonfim

68-69 The festivals of Bonfim last eight days culminating in the washing — 'an extraordinary mixture of paganism and Catholicism

56-57 During the feast of the washing of Bonfim, the « mothers of the saint » cover themselves with jewellery

72-73 The **Filhas de Santo** dressed all in white have offered to the saint the signs of purity — water and flowers

76 A priestess during a ceremony of **Umbunda**
77 Handbell

80-81 Two faces of « the possessed » the day of the feast of Iemanjá

100-101 Waiting for the departure of the regatta of **Saveiros** at the port of Santa Maria

84 Small doll signifying the goddess of the sea Iemanjá
85 Detail of a naive painting of Nair de Carvalho showing the procession of Iemanjá

102-103 Big and small, all the **saveiros** of the bay take part in this regatta in different categories

88 The statue of Iemanjá at Rio Vermelho
89 Offerings to the goddess are various : small statues, rice cakes, perfumes, flowers, soaps.

104 Ardour and passion are in every contestant
105 The only one of its kind, this sail of Asian influence stands out

92-93 All the offerings are put on board boats which leave in procession behind the boat of the goddess

106-107 While the **saveiro** heads towards victory, an **escuna** lowers his sails

96-97 The crowd surrounds a **Mãe de Santo** who is about to leave the beach of Rio Vermelho.

108-109 The procession of Nosso Senhor Bom Jesus dos Navigantes on the 1st January is one of the most beautiful sea processions imaginable.

98 Rich and poor pick all the flowers in the gardens of the town to offer them the **Mãe d'Agua**
99 A **Mãe de Santo** with an enviable head-dress

110-111 Against the background of dawn, the fishermen set out with their nets

112-113 La Puxada do Rede : in an arc, the men pull the net on the beach

126-127 The sugar cane factory : pulverising, pressing, cooking and finally the crystals of sugar

114-115 Close-up of a « miracle » fish during a **puxada**.

128 Packing
129 Weighing the sugar

116-117 Harvest of coconuts at Praia do Forte

130-131 **Piaçava**, a fibre resistant to heat and cold, is used to make brooms and in concrete where it replaces iron bars

132-133 Leaves of tobacco are dried then pounded to make the inside of a cigar

THE RECÔNCAVO

120-121 Firing the sugar cane fields

134-135 The leaves, dried in the sun, are pounded with the feet, selected, rolled and made into cigars before being boxed

124-125 The canes are then cut and piled up before being taken to the refinery

136-137 The purity and simplicity of the colonial style in a street of Cachoeira

138-139 The simple, coloured façades are brilliant in the sun

152 Small boy enjoying a mango
153 Cashew nuts

140-141 Small donkeys in the square of Cachoeira

156-157 Life in the market: a Bahian girl fries fritters of aca-rajé

142-143 The square of Dr. Milton in Cachoeira with the church of Santa Casa da Misericordia

THE THREE REGIONS OF THE
STATE OF BAHIA

144 Christ carrying the cross at the church/convent of the order of the Terceire do Carmo
145 The altar

160 Woman smoking a pipe in the market
161 The bird watches while this Bohemian reads a good yarn

146-147 7 christs of Chinese origin in the sacristy of the convent.

164-165 The bird is important in the Bahian life, immortalised here by the great artist Carybe

148-149 In the atelier of Los Loucos, José Cardoso de Araujo sculpts in wood

166-167 The weighing and loading of dende on the way to Nazare

168 Cutting the dende fruit
169 Stewing the bunches of fruit

180 Vivid whiteness of the cemetery of Santa Izabel in Mucugé
181 The long red road from Mucugé to Lençóis

170 Loading the press
171 Putting the dunde oil into bottles

182-183 Looking like the advertising panel of a handicraft shop, a semi-desolate landscape at the entrance of Milagres.

172 Cacao fruit on the tree, in the drier and the dried fruits
173 The inside of cacao fruit before drying

184 The verdant forests between Camacá and Nazaré
185 The pretty rooves of Lençóis, the city of diamonds

174-175 After drying and turning the clay many times, it goes on the wheel to be made into an object

186-187 Bahians loaded with buckets of water and flowers crossing the square of Horacio de Matos

176-177 A ceramic kiln in the tiny village of Maragojipe

188-189 At the church of Capela Senhor dos Passos, the washing takes place the day before the mass

178-179 Objects used during festivals
Usual objects waiting for customers

190-191 Three women returning home after the feast.

GLOSSARY

Agogô : percussion instrument composed of two small iron bells which are hit with a metal rod.

Atabaque : African drum used notably in Candomblé.

Azulejo : square of glazed earthenware with drawings often in blue (azul), used to decorate walls.

Batouque (Batuque) : the beating of the **atabaques** ; dance executed to the rhythm of these drums.

Berimbao (Berimbau) : resonance box made out of a water-bottle which is sounded by striking the metal with a rod.

Bumba-meu-boi : popular dance drame where the participants represent people, animals and fantastic creatures ; the central theme is the death and resurrection of an ox.

Caatinga : Indian word signifying « white forest », employed to describe the spiny, stunted, sparse vegetation of **Sertão**.

Cabocle (Caboclo) : god or spirit of the Indians.

Candomblé : African religion surviving in Bahia more or less in syncretism with Catholicism ; big celebrations to the **orishas** ; sanctuary where the celebrations take place.

Caranx (Xaréu) : caranx hippos, fish caught off the coast of Bahia during their seasonal migrations from the south to the north.

Carourou (Caruru) : a dish made up from the leaves of the plant of the same name cooked with fish and prawns in palm oil with pimento added.

Cuica : rudimentary musical instrument made out of a small cylindrical container over the opening of which is stretched a skin through which passes a rod. The sound comes from friction on the rod.

Echou (Exu) : messenger of the **orishas** and the spirit protector.

Efó : typical dish of Bahia and made up of various green vegetables cooked with dried prawns, palm oil and pimento.

Eugenia (Pitanqueira) : shrub with aromatic leaves which grows in sand dunes.

Fille de saint (Filhade-Santo) : a girl who has undergone the ritual of initiation. See also **Yawo**.

Iara : in the Indian beliefs, the siren of the rivers and the lakes.

Iná : one of the names of Yemanjá.

Janaina : one of the names of Yemanjá.

Mère de saint (Mãe-de-Santo) : high priestess of Candomblé.

Ogoum (Ogum) : the divinity of iron, forges, warriors, farmers and, in general, all those who use iron.

Orisha (Orixá) : the generic name for the intermediate gods between **Olorum**, the supreme god, and men.

Oshala (Oxalá) : god of the sky and of procreation.

Oshaloufan (Oxalufã) : ancient form of **Oxalá**.

Oshossi (Oxossi) : god of hunting.

Pagé (Pajé) : sorcerer priest or medecine man of the Indians.

Pégi (Péji) : altar of Candomblé where the stones consecrated to the **orishas** can be found.

Samba de roda : samba that the dancers perform by making a circle (**roda**).

Saveiro : sailboat used to transport cargo in All Saints Bay.

Sertão : semi-arid interior of north-east Brazil.

Umbanda : Afro-Brazilian form of spiritualism.

Vaquejada : Brazilian variation of rodeo.

Vatapá : typical dish of Bahia consisting of the following : fish (or chicken), dried prawns or fresh prawns, stale bread, flour made from ground nuts and grains of roasted cahews, palm oil, pimento and various seasonings.

Yansan (Iansã) : a female **orisha**, wife of Xangô, goddess of the winds and storms.

Yawo : see Fille de Saint.

Yemanjá (Iemanjá) : god of the sea, mother of the other **orhishas**.

Ynaé : one of the names of **Yemanjá**.

All the photographs of this book
were taken by Monique and Alain Draeger
and achieved with Leica cameras and lenses.

Monique and Alain Draeger's pictures
are available at the famous photograph agency
IMAGE BANK.

Jorge Amado wrote the texts and the diagram.

The illustrations made by Carlos Bastos
were taken out of the book
« Bahia de todos os santos »
by Jorge Amado

The painting featured on page 85
is due to Nair de Carvalho,
The painting on page 15 to Carybe.

The drawing on page 25 comes out
of the « Voyage pittoresque et historique au Bresil » by Debret

The dummy and the lay-out
were made by Guy Draeger

Transport was assured by Varig airline.

Editions d'Art Yvon
30, avenue Jean-Jaurès — 94115 Arcueil Cedex
FRANCE

I.S.B.N. 2.904226-01-X.